THE DINOSAUR JOKE BOOK

A Compendium of Pre-Hysteric Puns

By Artie Bennett

•

Illustrated by
Nate Evans

A Random House PICTUREBACK®

RANDOM HOUSE 🏠 **NEW YORK**

Text copyright © 1998 by Artie Bennett. Illustrations copyright © 1998 by Nate Evans.
All rights reserved under International and Pan-American Copyright Conventions. Published in the United States by Random House, Inc., New York,
and simultaneously in Canada by Random House of Canada Limited, Toronto.
http://www.randomhouse.com/
Library of Congress Cataloging-in-Publication Data
Bennett, Artie.
The dinosaur joke book : a compendium of pre-hysteric puns / by Artie Bennett ; illustrated by Nate Evans.
p.   cm. – (A Random House pictureback)
SUMMARY: An original collection of jokes and puns about dinosaurs.
ISBN: 0-679-88188-3 (pbk.)
1. Riddles, Juvenile.   2. Dinosaurs–Juvenile humor.
[1. Dinosaurs–Wit and humor.   2. Riddles.   3. Jokes.   4. Puns and punning.]   I. Evans, Nate, ill.   II. Title.
PN6371.5.B3875 1998 818'.5402–dc21 96-37477
Printed in the United States of America 10 9 8 7 6 5 4 3 2 1

Which dinosaur is always on time?
Pronto-saurus.

Which dinosaur spins around and around?

Tricera-tops.

What does a Pteranodon get after flying too long?

Ptired.

What do you call a dinosaur that eats automobiles?

A car-nivore.

Why were Stegosauruses popular at dinner parties?

They brought their own plates.

When were dinosaurs the friendliest?

During the Nice Age.

When were dinosaurs the sloppiest?
During the Mess-ozoic Era.

Where do dinosaurs still follow cavemen?

In the dictionary.

Which dinosaur loves to look up synonyms?

The Thesaurus.

Why did the duck-billed Hadrosaurus get in trouble?

He had a fowl mouth.

Why did the referee kick Ankylosaurus out of the football game?

He kept spiking the ball.

Which dinosaur knew shorthand?

Steno-saurus.

Why did the Ultrasaurus need a Band-Aid?

He had a dino-sore.

Why should you never slow-dance when Triceratops are around?

Because they keep horning in.

What did the boy Brachiosaurus and the
girl Brachiosaurus do on a date?

They necked.

What makes Tyranno-sore?
Too much Rex-ercise.

Who upheld the law during pre-hysteric times?

Tricera-cops.

Why did baby dinosaurs smell so bad?

Because their "eggs stinked."